ANOVA SOUS VIDE COOKBOOK FOR BEGINNERS

Tasty, Easy & Simple Recipes for Your Anova
Sous Vide to Make at Home Everyday

James Harris

CONTENTS

Stocks & Broths... 78

Sauces, Spices & Dips 84

INTRODUCTION

Tired of fattening food with the nutrients cooked out, or merely tired of paying big bucks at restaurants for healthy, delicious meals? Step into the world of juicy, simple, and healthy cooking with this gorgeous collection of 75 Sous Vide recipes.

Whether you're new to Sous Vide cooking and eager to learn or you're familiar with it and need to try your hand at some more recipes, this collection has scrumptious ideas to suit every taste and occasion. Start out with our basic methods and become a pro. We offer easy-to-follow cooking steps with ingredients that are readily available. Creating foods precisely like a chef couldn't be easier.

A QUICK INTRODUCTION TO SOUS VIDE

Sous Vide

Sous Vide is an old method of cooking meaning "cooking under vacuum" and expanded to mean cooking food in a vacuum under particular or controlled temperatures for a more extended period than you will in regular cooking.

This technique for the longest time had been one of the fanciest tricks in which restaurants made good food that looked and tasted very different from food made at home. Now, Sous Vide has become a household way of cooking with many Sous Vide cookers available and affordable just so that home-cooked foods can also be as good.

The results of Sous Vide food are known to be moderately cooked, leaving the food juicy, healthy, and beautiful to behold. They are made to prepare under vacuum, allowing their natural juices to do the job of cooking, hence the fresh look when ready. So, for example, a bunch of French beans may be Sous Vide and will turn out juicy to the taste and will maintain a naturally bright green color. With regular cooking, the French beans might be drier when chewed and will have a darker and dull green color when done.

Sous Vide cooking is usually complete in 5-steps:

1. Heating a water bath with a Sous Vide cooker in it, which is set at a particular temperature.

2. Preparing your food, seasoning it, oiling it, etc. as you will desire.

3. Placing the food in a sealable vacuum bag, releasing air from the bag, and sealing it.

    > **Tip:** Water Displacement Method: This process helps you release air efficiently from the bag when sealing it. Place the ingredient-filled bag halfway in the water bath, and air will naturally be released from the bag. Then seal it.

4. Placing the food in the water bath to cook for the desired time (see temperature guide below)

5. Searing the food with heat, if desired.

The essential utensils or equipment to Sous Vide with are:

- Sous Vide cooker - there are many brands and options on the market.

- Water bath - usually to be prepared in a deep container, however, some Sous Vide machines are designed to include this feature.

- Vacuum bag - food is placed in this bag and cooked under temperature. It has to be sealable and made of light plastic. A plastic zipper bag can serve this purpose well.

Cooking Sous Vide is such a fantastic method of cooking which allows you to prepare delicious, healthy food with no restrictions on the food type. It is, in short, a "set and go" kind of an approach to cooking. All that matters is ensuring that the temperatures, as well as cooking time, are set correctly, and voila, you will have fantastic food.

A temperature and time guide is provided here to help you make amazing dishes the Sous Vide way.

Sous Vide Temperature and Time Guide

Temperatures and Time can be adjusted as desired**

Food	Temperature	Time (MIN - MAX)
Eggs		
Soft Yolks	140 °F	1 HR
Hard-Cooked	160 °F	45 MIN -------------- 1 HR 15 MIN
Scrambled (5 eggs)	167 °F	45 MIN -------------- 1 HR 15 MIN
Sausages		
Soft and extra juicy	140 °F	45 MIN -------------- 4 HR
Firm	150 °F	45 MIN -------------- 4 HR
Springy	160 °F	45 MIN ------------ 4 HR
Hamburger		
Rare	115-123°F	30 MIN -------------- 2 HR 30 MIN
Medium Rare	124-129°F	30 MIN -------------- 2 HR 30 MIN
Medium	130-137°F	30 MIN -------------- 4 HR
Medium Well	138-144°F	30 MIN -------------- 4 HR
Medium Done	145-155°F	30 MIN -------------- 4 HR
Poultry (White Meat, Dark Meat, Duck - white meat)		
Medium Rare	140 °F	1 HR 30 MIN ------ 4 HR
Medium	145 °F - 150 °F	1 HR ----------------- 4 HR
Well Done	175 °F	1 HR ----------------- 4 HR
Red Meat		
Rare	120 °F	
Medium Rare	129 °F	1 HR---------------- 2 HR 30 MIN
Medium	140 °F	1 HR --------------- 4 HR
Medium Well	145 °F	1 HR --------------- 3 HR 30 MIN
Well Done	160 °F	3 HR---------------- 6 HR

Pork		
Medium Rare	135 °F	1 HR ---------------- 4 HR
Medium	140 °F	1 HR ---------------- 4 HR
Well Done	160 °F	1 HR ---------------- 4 HR
Fish & Seafood		
Tender but Translucent	110 °F	30 MIN
Tender and Flaky	125 °F	30 MIN --------------1 HR
Well Done	133 °F	30 MIN --------------1 HR 30 MIN
Green Vegetables		
Green Vegetables	183 °F	15 MIN ------------- 40 MIN

MEAT RECIPES

Garlic Tri-Tip Steak

Preparation time: 5 minutes
Cooking time: 2 hours 4 minutes
Serving: 2

Ingredients:

1 ½ lb Tri–tip Steak
Salt to taste
Pepper to taste
2 tbsp Soy Sauce
6 cloves Garlic, pre–roasted and crushed

Instructions:

1. Make a water bath, place a Sous Vide machine in it, and set it at 130 F.
2. Season the steak with pepper and salt and place it in a vacuum-sealable bag. Add the soy sauce.
3. Release air by the water displacement method and seal the bag.
4. Dip it in the water bath and set the timer for 2 hours.
5. Once the timer has stopped, remove and unseal the bag.
6. Heat a cast-iron pan over high heat, place the steak in and sear on both sides for 2 minutes each. Slice and serve in a salad.

Nutrition facts per serving: Calories 371, Total Fat 14.3g, Sodium 106mg, Potassium 86mg, Total Carbs 2g, Net Carbs 0g, Protein 37.7g

BBQ Rib Roast

Preparation time: 5 minutes
Cooking time: 1 hour 32 minutes
Servings: 4

Ingredients:

3 lb racks Beef Ribs, cut into 2
1 tsp Salt
1 tsp Black Pepper
½ cup Jalapeno-Tomato Blend
½ cup Barbecue Sauce

Instructions:

1. Make a water bath, place Sous Vide cooker in it, and set it at 140 F.
2. Rub salt and pepper graciously rib rack. Put the meat in a vacuum-sealable bags, release air and seal it.
3. Put the bag in the water bath and set the timer for 1 hour.
4. Once the timer has stopped, remove and unseal the bags. Mix the remaining listed ingredients. Let ribs cool for 30 minutes. Meanwhile, preheat a grill on medium heat.
5. Coat ribs with the jalapeno sauce and place it on the grill. Sear for 2 minutes on all sides.

Nutrition facts per serving: Calories 250, Total Fat 15g, Sodium 72mg, Potassium 318mg, Total Carbs 0g, Net Carbs 0g, Protein 26g

Celery Prime Rib with Herb Crust

Preparation time: 1 hour
Cooking time: 4 hours 15 minutes
Servings: 3

Ingredients:

1 ½ lb Rib Eye Steak, bone-in
½ tsp Black Pepper Powder
½ tsp Pink Pepper Powder
½ tbsp Celery Seeds, dried

1 tbsp Garlic Powder
2 sprigs Rosemary, minced
2 cups Beef Stock
1 Egg White

Instructions:

1. Rub salt into the meat and marinate for 1 hour. Make a water bath, place Sous Vide Cooker in it, and set to 130 F.

2. Place beef in a vacuum-sealable bag, release air by the water displacement method and seal the bag. Submerge the bag in the water bath.

3. Set the timer for 4 hours and cook. Once the timer has stopped, remove the bag and remove the beef. Pat dry beef and place aside.

4. Mix the black pepper powder, pink pepper powder, celery seeds, garlic powder, and rosemary. Brush the beef with the egg white.

5. Dip the beef in the celery seed mixture to coat graciously. Place beef on a baking sheet and bake in an oven for 15 minutes.

6. Remove and allow to cool on a cutting board. Gently slice the beef, cutting against the bone. Pour liquid in a vacuum bag and beef broth in a pan and bring to boil over medium heat. Discard floating fat or solids.

7. Place beef slices on a plate and drizzle sauce over it. Serve with a side of steamed green vegetables.

Nutrition facts per serving: Calories 112, Total Fat 7.27g, Sodium 91, Potassium 123mg, Total Carbs 0g, Net Carbs 0g, Protein 10.88g

Beef Steak with Tomato Roast

Preparation time: 5 minutes
Cooking time: 3 hours 15 minutes
Servings: 3

Ingredients:

1 lb Flank Steak

4 tbsp Olive Oil, divided into two

1 tbsp + 1 tsp Italian Seasoning

½ tsp Salt, divided into two

½ tsp Black Pepper, divided into two

4 cloves Garlic, 2 cloves crushed + 2 cloves whole

1 cup Cherry Tomatoes

1 tbsp Balsamic Vinegar

3 tbsp Parmesan Cheese, grated

Instructions:

1. Prepare a water bath, place Sous Vide cooker in it, and set to 129 F. Place the steak in a vacuum-sealable bag. Add half of the olive oil, Italian seasoning, black pepper, salt, and crushed garlic and rub gently.

2. Release air by the water displacement method and seal the bag. Submerge the bag in the water bath. Set the timer for 3 hours and cook 10 minutes before the timer has stopped, preheat an oven to 400 F.

3. In a bowl, toss tomatoes with the remaining listed ingredients except for the Parmesan cheese. Pour into a baking dish and place in the oven on the farthest rack from the fire. Bake for 15 minutes.

4. Once the Sous Vide timer has stopped, remove the bag, unseal and remove the steak. Place the steak on flat surface and sear both sides with a torch until golden brown. Cool steak and slice thinly. Serve steak with tomato roast. Garnish with Parmesan cheese.

Nutrition facts per serving: Calories 71, Total Fat 4.21g, Sodium 105, Potassium 86mg, Total Carbs 0g, Net Carbs 0g, Protein 24g

Thyme Veal with Mushroom Gravy

Preparation time: 5 minutes
Cooking time: 1 hour 33 minutes
Servings: 3

Ingredients:

½ lb Veal Cutlets
1 tsp Garlic Salt
1 cup Mushrooms, thinly sliced
⅓ cup Heavy Cream
2 Shallots, thinly sliced
1 tbsp Unsalted Butter
1 tsp Black Pepper Powder
1 sprig Thyme Leaves
1 tbsp Chopped Chives for garnishing

Instructions:

1. Prepare a water bath and place the Sous Vide Cooker in it. Set the Sous Vide Cooker to 129 F. Rub the cutlets with the garlic salt and place the veal with all the remaining listed ingredients except the chives in a vacuum-sealable bag.

2. Release the air by the water displacement method and seal it. Submerge it in the water bath. Set the timer for 1 hour 30 minutes and cook.

3. Once the timer has stopped, remove the bag and take out the veal unto a plate. Transfer the sauce to a pan, discard the thyme and simmer over low heat for 5 minutes. Add the veal and cook for 3 minutes. Garnish with chives.

4. Serve with a side of green vegetables or bread.

Nutritional facts per serving: Calories 100, Total Fat 4.85g, Sodium 190mg, Potassium 142mg, Total Carbs 1.36g, Net Carbs 1.35g, Protein 12.11g

Easy Veal Chops

Preparation time: 2 minutes
Cooking time: 2 hours 35 minutes
Servings: 4

Ingredients:

2 (16 oz) Veal Steaks
2 tsp Salt
2 tsp Black Pepper Powder
2 tbsp Olive Oil

Instructions:

1. Prepare a water bath, place the Sous Vide Cooker in it, and set it at 140 F. Rub the veal with pepper and salt and place in a Ziploc bag.
2. Release air by the water displacement method and seal the bag.
3. Submerge the bag in the water bath. Set the timer for 2 hours 30 minutes. Cook. Once the timer has stopped, remove and unseal the bag.
4. Remove the veal, pat dry using a napkin, and rub with the olive oil. Preheat a cast iron on high heat for 5 minutes.
5. Place the steak in and sear to deeply brown on both sides. Remove to a serving board. Serve with a side of salad.

Nutritional facts per serving: Calories 520, Total Fat 17g, Sodium 120mg, Total Carbs 3.4g, Net Carbs 2.5g, Protein 57g

Pork Ribs with Coconut-Peanut Sauce

Preparation time: 10 minutes
Cooking time: 8 hours 23 minutes
Servings: 3

Ingredients:

½ cup Coconut Milk, unsweetened
2 ½ tbsp Peanut Butter
2 tbsp Soy Sauce
1 tbsp Sugar
3 inches Fresh Lemongrass

1 ½ tbsp Pepper Sauce
1 ½ inch Ginger, peeled
3 cloves Garlic
2 ½ tsp Sesame Oil
13 oz Boneless Pork Ribs

Instructions:

1. Prepare a water bath and place a Sous Vide machine in it. Set the Sous Vide Machine at a temperature of 135 F. Blend all the listed ingredients in a blender except the pork ribs and cilantro until it's a smooth paste.

2. Place the ribs in a vacuum-sealable bag and add the blended sauce. Release air by the water displacement method and seal the bag. Place the bag in the water bath and set the timer for 8 hours.

3. Once the timer has stopped, take the bag out, unseal it and remove the ribs. Transfer it to a plate and keep it warm. Put a skillet over medium heat and pour in the sauce in the bag. Bring it to boil for 5 minutes, reduce the heat, and simmer for 12 minutes.

4. Add the ribs and coat it with the sauce. Simmer for 6 minutes. Serve with a side of steamed greens.

Nutrition facts per serving: Calories 495, Total Fat 27.4g, Sodium 99mg, Potassium 85mg, Total Carbs 1.22g, Net Carbs 1.21g, Protein 36.2g

Garlicky Pork Tenderloin

Preparation time: 15 minutes
Cooking time: 2 hours 10 minutes
Servings: 2

Ingredients:

2 tbsp Garlic Powder

2 tbsp Ground Cumin

2 tbsp Dried Thyme

2 tbsp Dried Rosemary

1 pinch Lime Sea Salt

2 (3-lb) Pork Tenderloin, silver skin removed

2 tbsp Olive Oil

2 tbsp Salt

3 tbsp Unsalted Butter

Instructions:

1. Make a water bath, place Sous Vide cooker in it, and set it at 140 F. Add the cumin, garlic powder, thyme, lime salt, rosemary, and lime salt to a bowl and mix evenly.

2. Brush the pork with olive oil, rub it with salt and cumin herb mixture.

3. Put the pork into two separate vacuum-sealable bags. Release air by the water displacement method and seal the bags. Submerge them in the water bath and set the timer for 2 hours.

4. Once the timer has stopped, remove and unseal the bag. Remove the pork and pat dry using a napkin. Discard the juice in the bag.

5. Preheat a cast iron pan over high heat and add the butter. Add the pork and sear to golden brown. Let the pork rest on a cutting board.

6. Cut them into 2-inch medallions.

Nutrition facts per serving: Calories 185, Total Fat 5.4g, Sodium 429mg, Potassium 491mg, Total Carbs 0g, Net Carbs 0g, Protein 31.5g

Savory Steaks with Mushroom Cream Sauce

Preparation time: 10 minutes
Cooking time: 1 hour 5 minutes
Servings: 3

Ingredients:

3 (6-oz) Boneless Sirloin Steaks
Salt and black pepper to taste
4 tsp Unsalted Butter
1 tbsp Olive Oil
6 oz White Mushrooms, quartered
2 large Shallots, minced
2 cloves Garlic, minced
½ cup Beef Stock
½ cup Heavy Cream
2 tsp Mustard Sauce
Thinly sliced Scallions for garnishing

Instructions:

1. Prepare a water bath, place Sous Vide cooker in it, and set to 135 °F.
2. Season the beef with pepper and salt and place them in a 3 separate vacuum-sealable bag.
3. Add 1 teaspoon of butter to each bag.
4. Release air by the water displacement method, seal and submerge the bag in the water bath.
5. Set the timer for 45 minutes.
6. Ten minutes before the timer stops, heat oil and the remaining butter in a skillet over medium heat.

7. Once the timer has stopped, remove and unseal the bag.
8. Remove the beef, pat dry, and place in the skillet.
9. Reserve the juices in the bags.
10. Sear on each side for 1 minute and transfer to a cutting board.
11. Slice them and place them aside.
12. In the same skillet, add the shallots and mushrooms.
13. Cook for 10 minutes and add the garlic. Cook for 1 minute.
14. Add the stock and reserved juices. Simmer for 3 minutes.
15. Add the heavy cream, bring to a boil on high heat and reduce to low heat after 5 minutes.
16. Turn the heat off and stir in the mustard sauce.
17. Place the steak on a plate, top with mushroom sauce and garnish with scallions.

Nutrition facts per serving: Calories 220, Total Fat 6.8g, Sodium 599mg, Potassium 442mg, Total Carbs 3.9g, Net Carbs 3.7g, Protein 19.9g

Awesome Jerk Pork Ribs

Preparation time: 15 minutes
Cooking time: 20 hours 15 minutes
Servings: 6

Ingredients:

5 lb (2) Baby Back Pork Ribs, full racks
½ cup Jerk Seasoning Mix

Instructions:

1. Make a water bath, place a Sous Vide cooker in it, and set it at 145°F.
2. Cut the racks into halves and season them with half the jerk seasoning.
3. Place the racks in 4 separate vacuum-sealable racks.
4. Release air by the water displacement method, seal and submerge the bags in the water bath. Set the timer for 20 hours to cook.
5. Cover the water bath with a bag to reduce evaporation and add water every 3 hours to avoid the water drying out.
6. Once the timer has stopped, remove and unseal the bag.
7. Transfer the ribs to a foiled baking sheet and preheat a broiler to high.
8. Rub the ribs with the remaining jerk seasoning and place them in the broiler.
9. Broil for 5 minutes. Slice into single ribs.

Nutrition facts per serving: Calories 380, Total Fat 21.5g, Sodium 320mg, Total Carbs 4g, Net Carbs 4g, Protein 21.2g

Tasty Beef Pear Steak

Preparation time: 5 minutes
Cooking time: 3 hours 3 minutes
Servings: 3

Ingredients:

3 (6 oz) Beef Pear Steaks
2 tbsp Olive Oil
4 tbsp Unsalted Butter
4 cloves Garlic, crushed
4 sprigs Fresh Thyme

Instructions:

1. Make a water bath, place the Sous Vide Cooker in it, and set to 135°F.
2. Season the beef with salt and place beef in 3 vacuum-sealable bags.
3. Release air by the water displacement method and seal bag.
4. Submerge the bag in the water bath. Set the timer for 3 hours and cook.
5. Once the timer has stopped, remove the beef, pat dry, and season with pepper and salt.
6. Add oil to skillet and preheat it on medium heat until it starts to smoke.
7. Add the steaks, butter, garlic, and thyme. Sear for 3 minutes on both side.
8. Baste with some more butter as you cook.
9. Slice steaks into desired slices.

Nutrition facts per serving: Calories 360, Total Fat 11.5g, Sodium 520mg, Total Carbs 5g, Net Carbs 5g, Protein 27g

Quick Sirloin Steak with Mashed Potatoes

Preparation time: 15 minutes
Cooking time: 1 hour 20 minutes
Servings: 4

Ingredients:

4 Sirloin Steaks
2 lbs of Potatoes, diced
Salt and Pepper to taste
4 tbsp Butter
Olive oil for searing

Instructions:

1. Make a water bath, place a Sous Vide cooker in it, and set it to 128 F. Season steaks with pepper and salt and place in a vacuum-sealable bag.
2. Release air by the water displacement method, seal and submerge the bag in the water bath. Set the timer for 1 hour.
3. Place the potatoes in boiling water and cook until tender for about 20 minutes.
4. Strain the potatoes and place in a mixing bowl. Add butter and mash them. Season with pepper and salt.
5. Once the timer has stopped, remove and unseal the bags. Remove the steaks from the bag and pat dry. Re-season as desired.
6. Sear the steaks in a pan with oil over medium heat for about 2 minutes on each side. Serve steaks with mashed turnips.

Nutrition facts per serving: Calories 394, Total Fat 14.8, Sodium 982mg, Potassium 450mg, Total Carbs 35.7g, Net Carbs 21.7g, Protein 21.3g

Delicious Pork Chops with Mushroom Sauce

Preparation time: 1 minute
Cooking time: 65 minutes
Servings: 3

Ingredients:

3 (8 oz) Pork Chops

Black Pepper Powder to taste

3 tbsp Butter, unsalted

6 oz Mushrooms

½ cup Beef Stock

2 tbsp Worcestershire Sauce

3 tbsp Garlic Chives, chopped for garnishing

Instructions:

1. Make a water bath, place a Sous Vide cooker in it, and set it at 140 F.
2. Rub pork chops with salt and pepper and place them in a vacuum-sealable bag. Release air by the water displacement method, seal and submerge the bag in the water bath. Set the timer for 55 minutes.
3. Once the timer has stopped, remove and unseal the bag.
4. Remove the pork and pat it dry using a napkin. Discard the juices.
5. Place a skillet over medium heat and add 1 tablespoon butter.
6. Once the butter has melted, add pork and sear for 2 minutes on both sides. Place aside.
7. With the skillet still over the heat, add the mushrooms and cook for 5 minutes.
8. Turn heat off, add the remaining butter and swirl until butter melts. Season with pepper and salt. Serve pork chops with mushroom sauce over it.

Nutrition facts per serving: Calories 297, Total Fat 18g, Sodium 529mg, Total Carbs 11g, Net Carbs 11g, Protein 25.7 g

Barbecued Pork Ribs

Preparation time: 2 minutes
Cooking time: 1 hour 5 minutes
Servings: 4

Ingredients:

1 lb Pork Ribs
1 tsp Garlic Powder
1 tsp Black Pepper Powder
1 tsp Salt
1 cup BBQ Sauce (see recipe above)

Instructions:

1. Make a water bath, place Sous Vide cooker in it, and set it at 140 F.
2. Rub salt and pepper graciously on the pork ribs.
3. Put the ribs in a vacuum-sealable bag, release air and seal it.
4. Put it in the water and set the timer for 1 hour.
5. Once the timer has stopped, remove and unseal the bag.
6. Remove ribs and coat with BBQ sauce. Place aside.
7. Preheat a grill.
8. Once it is hot, sear the ribs all around for 5 minutes.
9. Serve with a dip of choice.

Nutrition facts per serving: Calories 290, Total Fat 17g, Sodium 850mg, Total Carbs 15g, Net Carbs 14g, Protein 14g

Garlic Roasted Pork Neck

Preparation time: 15 minutes
Cooking time: 1 hour 15 minutes
Servings: 8

Ingredients:

2 lb Pork Neck, boneless and sliced into 2

4 tbsp Olive Oil

2 tsp Soy Sauce

2 tbsp Barbecue Sauce

2 tbsp Sugar

4 sprigs Rosemary, leaves removed

4 sprigs Thyme, leaves removed

2 cloves Garlic, minced

¼ tsp Salt

¼ tsp White Pepper Powder

¼ tsp Red Pepper Flakes

Instructions:

1. Make a water bath, place Sous Vide cooker in it, and set it at 140 F.
2. Rub salt and pepper graciously on the pork.
3. Put the meat in 2 separate vacuum-sealable bags, release air and seal them.
4. Put them in the water bath and set the timer for 1 hour.
5. Once the timer has stopped, remove and unseal the bags. Mix the remaining listed ingredients. Preheat oven to 425 F.
6. Put the pork on a roasting pan and rub soy sauce mixture generously into the pork. Roast it in the oven for 15 minutes. Let pork cool and slice it.
7. Serve with a side of steamed greens.

Nutrition facts per serving: Calories 315, Protein 28.7g, Total Fat 20.8g, Total Carbs 0g, Net Carbs 0g, Protein 17.5g

Herb Crusted Lamb Rack

Preparation time: 15 minutes
Cooking time: 3 hours 24 minutes
Servings: 6

Ingredients:

Lamb Rack:
3 large Racks of Lamb
Salt to taste
3 tsp Black Pepper Powder
1 sprig Rosemary
2 tbsp Olive Oil

Herb Crust:
2 tbsp Fresh Rosemary Leaves
½ cup Macadamia Nuts
2 tbsp Dijon Mustard
½ cup Fresh Parsley
2 tbsp Fresh Thyme Leaves
2 tbsp Lemon Zest
2 cloves Garlic
2 Egg Whites

Instructions:

1. Make a water bath, place the Sous Vide Cooker in it, and set to 140 F.
2. Pat dry the lamb using a napkin and rub the meat with salt and black pepper.
3. Place a pan over medium heat and add olive oil.
4. Once it has heated, sear the lamb on both sides for 2 minutes.

5. Remove and place aside.Add garlic and rosemary to the pan, toast for 2 minutes and pour over the lamb.

6. Leave lamb to sit and cool for 5 minutes.

7. Place lamb, garlic, and rosemary in a vacuum-sealable bag, release air by the water displacement method and seal the bag.

8. Submerge the bag in the water bath.

9. Set the timer to cook for 3 hours.Once the timer has stopped, remove the bag, unseal it and take out the lamb.

10. Whisk the egg whites and place aside.

11. Blend the remaining listed herb crust ingredients using a blender and place aside.

12. Pat dry the lamb using a napkin and brush the meat with the egg whites.

13. Dip into the herb mixture and coat graciously.

14. Place the lamb racks with crust side up on a baking sheet.

15. Bake in the oven for 15 minutes.

16. Gently slice each cutlet using a sharp knife.

17. Serve with a side of pureed vegetables.

Nutrition facts per serving: Calories 250, Total Fat 20g, Sodium 190mg, Total Carbs 0g, Net Carbs 0g, Protein 14g

Cheesy Lamb Ribs

Preparation time: 5 minutes
Cooking time: 4 hours
Servings: 2

Ingredients:

Ribs:

2 half racks Lamb Ribs
2 tbsp Vegetable Oil
1 clove Garlic, minced
2 tbsp Rosemary Leaves, chopped

1 tbsp Fennel Pollen
½ tsp Black Pepper Powder
½ tsp Cayenne Pepper
Salt to taste

To Garnish:

8 oz Goat Cheese, crumbled
2 oz Roasted Walnuts, chopped

3 tbsp Parsley, chopped

Instructions:

1. Make a water bath, place the Sous Vide Cooker in it, and set to 134 F.
2. Mix the listed lamb ingredients except for the lamb. Pat dry the lamb using a napkin and rub the meat with the spice mixture.
3. Place the meat in a vacuum-sealable bag, release air by the water displacement method, seal and submerge in the water bath. Set the timer for 4 hours. Once the timer has stopped, remove the bag and remove the lamb.
4. Oil and preheat a grill on high heat. Place the lamb on it and sear to become golden brown. Cut the ribs between the bones. Garnish with goat cheese, walnuts and parsley. Serve with a hot sauce dip.

Nutritional facts per serving: Calories 165, Total Fat 13.56g, Sodium 109mg, Potassium 124mg, Total Carbs 1g, Net Carbs 1g, Protein 10.14g

BBQ Shredded Roast

Preparation time: 1 minute
Cooking time: 16 hours 15 minutes
Servings: 3

Ingredients:

1 medium Chuck Roast

BBQ Seasoning, of your choice

2 cups Beef Stock

Instructions:

1. Make a water bath, place the Sous Vide Cooker in it, and set to 165 F.
2. Preheat a grill. Pat dry the meat using a napkin and rub with BBQ seasoning. Set aside for 15 minutes.
3. Place the meat on the grill and roast for 2 hours on each side, spritzing with beef stock each hour.
4. Place meat in a vacuum-sealable bag, release air by the water displacement method and seal the bag
5. Submerge bag in the water bath. Set the timer for 14 hours and cook.
6. Once the timer has stopped, remove the bag and unseal it.
7. Remove the meat and shred it. Serve it in a sandwich made with bread.

Nutrition facts per serving: Calories 456, Total Fat 23.6g, Sodium 46mg, Potassium 61mg, Total Carbs 0g, Net Carbs 0g, Protein 35.6g

Cilantro Lamb Roast

Preparation time: 5 minutes
Cooking time: 2 hours 46 minutes
Servings: 6

Ingredients:

1 ½ tbsp Canola Oil

1 tbsp Black Mustard Seeds

1 tsp Cumin Seeds

Salt to taste

Black Pepper to taste

4 lb Butterflied Lamb Leg

½ cup Mint Leaves, chopped

½ cup Cilantro Leaves, chopped

1 Shallot, minced

1 clove Garlic, minced

2 Red Jalapenos, minced

1 tbsp Red Wine Vinegar

1 ½ tbsp Olive Oil

Instructions:

1. Place a skillet over low heat on a stovetop.
2. Add ½ tablespoon of olive oil; once it has heated add cumin and mustard seeds and cook for 1 minute.
3. Turn off heat and transfer seeds to a bowl. Add salt and black pepper. Mix.
4. Spread half of the spice mixture inside the lamb leg and roll it.
5. Secure with a butcher's twine at 1- inch intervals.
6. Season with salt and pepper and massage.

7. Spread half of the spice mixture evenly over inside of lamb leg, then carefully roll it back up. Make a water bath and place the Sous Vide Cooker in it.

8. Set the Sous Vide cooker at145 F.

9. Place the lamb leg in vacuum-sealable bag, release air by the water displacement method, seal and submerge it in the water bath.

10. Set the timer for 2 hours 45 minutes and cook.

11. Make the sauce; add to the cumin mustard mixture shallot, cilantro, garlic, red wine vinegar, mint, red chili. Mix and season with salt and pepper. Place aside.

12. Once the Sous Vide timer has stopped, remove and unseal the bag.

13. Remove the lamb and pat dry using a napkin.

14. Add canola oil to cast iron, preheat over high heat for 10 minutes.

15. Add lamb and sear to brown on both sides.

16. Remove twine and slice lamb.

17. Serve with sauce.

Nutrition facts per serving Calories 37, Total Fat 2.54g, Sodium 32mg, Potassium 39mg, Total Carbs 0g, Net Carbs 0g, Protein 3.35g

Chimichurri Lamb Chops

Preparation time: 25 minutes
Cooking time: 3 hours 30 minutes
Servings:

Ingredients:

Lamb Chops:

3 Lamb Racks, frenched

3 cloves Garlic, crushed

⅓ tsp Salt

1 tsp Black Pepper Powder

Basil Chimichurri:

1 ½ cups Fresh Basil, finely chopped

2 Banana Shallots, diced

3 cloves Garlic, minced

1 tsp Red Pepper Flakes

½ cup Olive Oil

3 tbsp Red Wine Vinegar

½ tsp Salt

½ tsp Black Pepper

Instructions:

1. Prepare a water bath and place the Sous Vide Cooker in it.
2. Set the Sous Vide Cooker to 140 F.
3. Pat dry the racks with a napkin and rub with pepper and salt.
4. Place meat and garlic in a vacuum-sealable bag, release air by water displacement method and seal the bag.

5. Submerge the bag in the water bath.

6. Set the timer for 2 hours and cook.

7. Make the basil chimichurri: mix all the listed ingredients in a bowl.

8. Cover with cling film and refrigerate for 1 hour 30 minutes.

9. Once the Sous Vide timer has stopped, remove the bag and open it.

10. Remove the lamb and pat dry using a napkin.

11. Sear with a torch to a golden brown.

12. Pour the basil chimichurri on the lamb.

13. Serve with a side of steamed greens.

Nutrition facts per serving: Calories 226, Total Fat 17.55g, Sodium 281mg, Potassium 184mg, Total Carbs 0g, Net Carbs 0g, Protein 15.86g

Thyme & Rosemary Lamb Shoulder

Preparation time: 2 minutes

Cooking time: 4 hours 12 minutes

Servings: 3

Ingredients:

1 lb. Lamb Shoulder, deboned

1 tsp Salt

2 tsp Black Pepper

2 tbsp Olive Oil

1 Garlic Clove, crushed

1 sprig Thyme

1 sprig Rosemary

Instructions:

1. Prepare a water bath and place the Sous Vide Cooker in it.
2. Set the Sous Vide Cooker to 145 F. Pat dry the lamb shoulders using a napkin and rub with pepper and salt.
3. Place the lamb and the remaining listed ingredients in a vacuum-sealable bag.
4. Release air by the water displacement method, seal and submerge the bag in the water bath. Set the timer for 4 hours.
5. Once the timer has stopped, remove the bag and transfer the lamb shoulders to baking dish.
6. Strain the juices into a saucepan and cook over medium heat for 2 minutes.
7. Preheat a grill for 10 minutes and grill the shoulder until golden brown and crispy. Serve the lamb shoulder and sauce with a side of buttered greens.

Nutritional facts per serving: Calories 39, Total Fat 2.78, Sodium 32mg, Potassium 35mg, Total Carbs 0g, Net Carbs 0g, Protein 3.14g

POULTRY RECIPES

Celery Whole Chicken

Preparation time: 10 minutes
Cooking time: 6 hours
Serving: 6

Ingredients:

1 (5 lb) Whole Chicken, trussed
5 cups Chicken Stock
3 cups Mixed Bell Peppers, diced
3 cups Celery, diced

3 cups Leeks, diced
1 ¼ tsp Salt
1 ¼ tsp Black Peppercorns
2 Bay Leaves

Instructions:

8. Make a water bath, place a Sous Vide machine in it, and set it at 150 F. Season the chicken with salt.

9. Place all the listed ingredients and chicken in a sizable vacuum-sealable bag. Release air by the water displacement method and seal the vacuum bag. Drop the bag in water bath and set the timer for 7 hours.

10. Cover the water with a plastic bag to reduce evaporation and water every 2 hours to the bath.

11. Once the timer has stopped, remove and unseal the bag.

12. Preheat a broiler, carefully remove the chicken and pat it dry.

13. Place the chicken in the broiler and broil it until the skin is golden brown.

14. Rest the chicken for 8 minutes, slice and serve.

Nutrition facts per serving: Calories 210, Total Fat 15g, Sodium 200mg, Total Carbs 0g, Net Carbs 0g, Protein 19g

Sage Turkey Roulade

Preparation time: 20 minutes
Cooking time: 3 hours
Servings: 6

Ingredients:

3 tbsp Olive Oil

2 small Yellow Onions, diced

2 stalks Celery, diced

3 tbsp Ground Sage

2 Lemons' Zest and Juice

3 cups Turkey Stuffing Mix

2 cups Turkey or Chicken Stock

5 lb halved Turkey Breast

Instructions:

1. Place a pan over medium heat, add olive oil, onion, and celery.
2. Sauté for 2 minutes.
3. Add the lemon juice, zest, and sage until the lemon juice reduces.
4. In a bowl, pour the stuffing mixture and add the cooked sage mixture. Mix it with your hands.
5. Add in the stock gently, while mixing with your hand until ingredients hold together well and are not runny.
6. Gently remove the turkey meat skin and lay it on a plastic wrap.
7. Remove bones and discard.
8. Place the turkey breast on the skin and lay second layer of plastic wrap on the turkey breast.
9. Flatten it to 1 - inch of thickness using a rolling pin.

10. Remove the plastic wrap on top and spread the stuffing on the flattened turkey, leaving ½ inch space around the edges.

11. Starting at the narrow side, roll the turkey like a pastry roll and drape the extra skin on the turkey. Secure the roll with butcher's twine.

12. Wrap the turkey roll in the broader plastic wrap and twist the ends to secure the roll, which should form a tight cylinder.

13. Place the roll in a vacuum-sealable bag, release air and seal the bag. Refrigerate it for 40 minutes.

14. Make a water bath, place a Sous Vide cooker in it, and set it at 155 F.

15. Place the turkey roll in the water bath and set the timer for 4 hours.

16. Once the timer has stopped, remove the bag and unseal it.

17. Preheat an oven to 400 F, remove the plastic wrap from the turkey and place it on a baking dish with skin side up.

18. Roast for 15 minutes. Slice in rounds.

19. Serve with a creamy sauce and steamed veggies.

Nutrition facts per serving: Calories 210, Total Fat 5g, Sodium 560mg, Total Carbs 20g, Net Carbs1g, Protein 20g

Cheesy Crusted Chicken Breast

Preparation time: 15 minutes
Cooking time: 51 minutes
Servings: 4

Ingredients:

2 Chicken Breast, skinless and boneless
1 ½ cups Basil Pesto
½ cup Macadamia Nuts, grounded
¼ cup Parmesan Cheese, grated
3 tbsp Olive Oil

Instructions:

1. Make a water bath, place Sous Vide cooker in it, and set it at 65 F. Cut chicken into bite-size pieces and coat with pesto.
2. Place the chicken flat in two separate vacuum bags without overlapping them.
3. Release air by the water displacement method and seal the bags. Submerge them in the water bath and set the timer for 50 minutes.
4. Once the timer has stopped, remove and unseal the bag.
5. Transfer the chicken pieces to a plate without the juices. Sprinkle macadamia nuts and cheese over it and coat well.
6. Set a skillet over high heat, add olive oil. Once the oil has heated, quickly fry the coated chicken for 1 minute all around.
7. Drain fat. Serve as a starter dish.

Nutrition facts per serving: Calories 165, Total Fat 3.6g, Sodium 74mg, Potassium 318mg, Total Carbs 15g, Net Carbs 14g, Protein 31g

Thyme Chicken Thighs with Lemon

Preparation time: 5 minutes
Cooking time: 25 minutes
Servings: 3

Ingredients:

3 Chicken Thighs
Salt to taste
Pepper to taste
3 slices Lemon
3 sprigs Thyme
3 tbsp Olive Oil for searing

Instructions:

1. Make a water bath, place a Sous Vide cooker in it, and set it at 165 F.
2. Season the chicken with salt and pepper. Place a slice of lemon on each chicken and top it with each thyme sprig.
3. Place them in a vacuum-sealable bag, release air by the water displacement method and seal the bag.
4. Submerge the bag in the water bag and set the timer for 2 hours.
5. Once the timer has stopped, remove and unseal the bag.
6. Heat olive oil in a cast iron pan over high heat.
7. Place the chicken thighs, skin down in the skillet and sear until golden brown. Garnish with extra lemon wedges. Serve with a side of cauli rice.

Nutrition facts per serving: Calories 603, Protein 21g, Total Fat 20g, Sodium 89mg, Total Carbs 3g, Net Carbs 1g, Protein 25g

Easy Duck Breast

Preparation time: 1 minute
Cooking time: 1 hour 5 minutes
Servings: 3

Ingredients:

3 (6 oz) Duck Breast, skin on
3 tsp Thyme Leaves
2 tsp Olive Oil

Ingredients:

1. Make crosswise strips on the ducks and without cutting into the meat.
2. Season the skin with salt and the meat side with thyme, pepper, and salt.
3. Place the duck breasts in 3 separate vacuum-sealable bags. Release air and seal the bag. Refrigerate for 1 hour.
4. Make a water bath, place a Sous Vide cooker in it, and set it at 135 F.
5. Remove the bag from the refrigerator and submerge the bag in the water bath. Set the timer for 1 hour.
6. Once the timer has stopped, remove and unseal the bag.
7. Set a skillet over medium heat, add olive oil. Once it has heated, add duck and sear until skin renders and meat is golden brown.
8. Remove and let sit for 3 minutes and then slice.
9. Serve with a side of braised beetroot (see recipe in the vegetable segment).

Nutrition facts per serving: Calories 242, Protein 29.4g, Total Fat 13.02g, Sodium 101mg, Total Carbs 0g , Net Carbs 0g

Macadamia Chicken Patties

Preparation time: 10 minutes
Cooking time: 3 hours 5 minutes
Servings: 5

Ingredients:

½ lb Chicken Breast, skinless and boneless

½ cup Macadamia Nuts, grounded

⅓ cup Olive Oil Mayonnaise

3 Green Onions, finely chopped

2 tbsp Lemon Juice

⅛ tsp Black Pepper

3 tbsp Olive Oil

Instructions:

1. Make a water bath, place a Sous Vide cooker in it, and set it at 165 F.
2. Put chicken in a vacuum-sealable bag, release air by the water displacement method and seal it. Put the bag in the water bath and set the timer for 3 hours. Once the timer has stopped, remove and unseal the bag.
3. Shred the chicken using two forks. In a bowl, add the chicken and all the remaining listed ingredients except olive oil. Mix evenly. Make patties and set aside. Heat olive oil in a skillet over medium heat.
4. Add patties and fry to golden brown on both sides and heated through.
5. Serve in sandwiches made with bread.

Nutrition facts per serving: Calories 165, Total Fat 3.6g, Sodium 74mg, Total Carbs 10g, Net Carbs 10g, Protein 31g

Spicy Chicken Thighs

Preparation time: 2 minutes
Cooking time: 2 hours 40 minutes
Servings: 6

Ingredients:

1 lb Chicken Thighs, bone-in
3 tbsp Butter
1 tbsp Cayenne Pepper
Salt to taste

Instructions:

1. Make a water bath, place a Sous Vide cooker in it, and set it at 165 F.
2. Season the chicken with pepper and salt.
3. Place chicken with one tablespoon of butter in a vacuum-sealable bag.
4. Release air by the water displacement method, seal and submerge the bag in the water bath. Set the timer for 2 hours 30 minutes.
5. Once the timer has stopped, remove the bag and unseal it.
6. Preheat a grill and melt the remaining butter in a microwave.
7. Oil the grill grate with some of the butter and brush the chicken with the remaining butter.
8. Sear until dark brown color is achieved.
9. Serve as a snack.

Nutrition facts per serving: Calories 260 , Total Fat 18g, Sodium 460mg, Potassium 51mg, Total Carbs 8g, Net Carbs 7g, Protein 14g

Simple No-sear Chicken Breast

Preparation time: 5 minutes

Cooking time: 1 hour

Servings: 3

Ingredients:

1 lb Chicken Breasts, boneless

Salt to taste

Pepper to taste

1 tsp Garlic Powder

Instructions:

1. Make a water bath, place a Sous Vide machine in it, and set it to 150 F.
2. Pat dry the chicken breasts and season with salt, garlic powder, and pepper.
3. Put the chicken in a vacuum-sealable bag, release air by the water displacement method and seal it.
4. Place it in the water and set the timer to cook for 1 hour.
5. Once the timer has stopped, remove and unseal the bag.
6. Remove the chicken and chill it for later use.

Nutrition facts per serving: Calories 164, Total Fat 6.48g, Sodium 330mg, Potassium 204mg, Total Carbs 0g, Net Carbs 0g, Protein 24.82g

Spicy & Sweet Chicken Drumsticks

Preparation time: 10 minutes
Cooking time: 2 hours 10 minutes
Servings: 3

Ingredients:

½ tbsp. Sugar
½ cup Soy Sauce
2 ½ tsp Ginger, chopped
2 ½ tsp Garlic, chopped
2 ½ tsp Red Chili Puree

¼ lb small Chicken Drumsticks, skinless
2 tbsp Olive Oil
2 tbsp Sesame Seeds to garnish
1 Scallion, chopped to garnish

Instructions:

1. Make a water bath, place a Sous Vide cooker in it, and set it at 165 F.
2. Rub chicken with salt and pepper. Put chicken in a vacuum-sealable bag, release air by water displacement method and seal it.
3. Put the bag in the water bath and set the timer for 2 hours.
4. Once the timer has stopped, remove and unseal the bag.
5. In a bowl, mix the remaining listed ingredients except for olive oil.
6. Place aside. Heat oil in a skillet over medium heat, add chicken.
7. Once they brown slightly on both sides, add the sauce and coat the chicken with it. Cook for 10 minutes.
8. Garnish with sesame and scallions. Serve with a side of cauliflower rice.

Nutrition facts per serving: Calories 81, Total Fat 5.4g, Sodium 113mg, Total Carbs 0g, Net Carbs 0g, Protein 7.46g

FISH & SEAFOOD

Ginger-Sweet Salmon

Preparation time: 3 minutes
Cooking time: 30 minutes
Servings: 4

Ingredients:

4 Salmon Fillets, with skin
2 tsp Sesame Oil
1 ½ Olive Oil
2 tbsp Ginger, grated
2 tbsp Sugar

Instructions:

1. Make a water bath, place a Sous Vide cooker in it, and set it at 124 F. Season salmon with salt and pepper. Place the remaining listed ingredient in a bowl and mix.
2. Place salmon and sugar mixture into two vacuum-sealable bags, release air by the water displacement method, seal and submerge the bag in the water bath. Set the timer for 30 minutes.
3. Once the timer has stopped, remove and unseal the bag.
4. Place a skillet over medium heat, place a piece of parchment paper at its bottom and let the skillet preheat. Add the salmon, skin down to the skillet, and sear for 1 minute each. Serve with a side of buttered broccoli.

Nutrition facts per serving: Calories 208, Total Fat 13g, Sodium 59mg, Potassium 363mg, Total Carbs 10g, Net Carbs 10g, Protein 20g

Mustardy Salmon

Preparation time: 35 minutes
Cooking time: 46 minutes
Servings: 3

Ingredients:

3 Salmon Filets, skinless
1 tbsp Sugar
2 tsp Smoked Paprika
1 tsp Mustard Powder

Instructions:

1. Prepare a water bath, place a Sous Vide machine in it, and set it to 115 F.
2. Season the salmon with 1 teaspoon of salt and place it in a zipper bag. Refrigerate for 30 minutes.
3. In a bowl, mix the sugar, smoked salt, remaining salt, and mustard powder and mix to combine.
4. Remove the salmon from the fridge and rub with the sugar.
5. Place salmon in a vacuum-sealable bag, release air by the water displacement method and seal the bag.
6. Submerge the bag in the water bath and set the timer for 45 minutes.
7. Once the timer has stopped, remove the bag and unseal it.
8. Remove the salmon and pat it dry using a napkin.
9. Place a non – stick skillet over medium heat, add the salmon and sear it for 30 seconds. Serve with a side of steamed greens.

Nutrition facts per serving: Calories 357, Total Fat 13.72g, Sodium 950mg, Potassium 603mg, Total Carbs 2g, Net Carbs 2g, Protein 40.9g

Buttered Sole

Preparation time: 2 minutes
Cooking time: 30 minutes
Servings: 3

Ingredients:

3 Sole Filets
1 ½ tbsp Unsalted Butter
¼ cup Lemon Juice
½ tsp Lemon Zest
Lemon Pepper to taste
1 sprig Parsley for garnishing

Instructions:

1. Make a water bath, place a Sous Vide cooker in it, and set it at 132 F.
2. Pat dry the sole and place in 3 separate vacuum-sealable bags.
3. Release air by the water displacement method and seal the bags.
4. Submerge them in the water bath and set the timer for 30 minutes.
5. Place a small pan over medium heat, add the butter. Once it has melted, remove it from the heat. Add lemon juice and lemon zest and stir.
6. Once the Sous Vide timer has stopped, remove and unseal the bag.
7. Transfer the sole filets to serving plates, drizzle butter sauce over it and garnish with parsley. Serve with a side of steam green vegetables.

Nutrition facts per serving: Calories 70, Total Fat 2g, Sodium 310mg, Total Carbs 0g, Net Carbs 0g, Protein 13g

Savory Homemade Tilapia

Preparation time: 1 minute
Cooking time: 1 hour 10 minutes
Servings: 3

Ingredients

3 (4 oz) Tilapia Filets
3 tbsp Butter
1 tbsp Apple Cider Vinegar
Salt for seasoning
Pepper for seasoning

Instructions:

1. Make a water bath, place a Sous Vide cooker in it, and set it at 124 F.
2. Season the tilapia with pepper and salt and place in a vacuum-sealable bag.
3. Release air by the water displacement method and seal the bag.
4. Submerge it in the water bath and set the timer for 1 hour.
5. Once the timer has stopped, remove and unseal the bag.
6. Put a skillet over medium heat and add butter and vinegar.
7. Simmer and stir continually to reduce vinegar by half. Add the tilapia and sear slightly. Season with salt and pepper as desired.
8. Serve with a side of buttered vegetables.

Nutrition facts per serving: Calories 129, Total Fat 2.7g, Sodium 56mg, Potassium 380mg, Total Carbs 0g, Net Carbs 0g, Protein 26g

Effortless Mackerel

Preparation time: 15 minutes
Cooking time: 50 minutes
Servings: 3

Ingredients:

3 Mackerel Filets, heads removed

3 tbsp Curry Paste

1 tbsp Olive Oil

Salt to season

Pepper to season

Instructions:

1. Make a water bath, place a Sous Vide cooker in it, and set it at 120 F.
2. Season the mackerel with pepper and salt and place in a vacuum-sealable bag.
3. Release air by the water displacement method, seal and submerge it in the water bath, and set the timer for 40 minutes.
4. Once the timer has stopped, remove and unseal the bag.
5. Set a skillet over medium heat, add olive oil.
6. Meanwhile, coat the mackerel with the curry powder (do not pat the mackerel dry)
7. Once it has heated, add the mackerel and sear until golden brown. Serve with a side of steamed green leafy vegetables.

Nutrition facts per serving: Calories 186, Total Fat 14g, Sodium 80mg, Potassium 268mg, Total Carbs 0.5g, Net Carbs 0.5g, Protein 14g

Dilled Grouper

Preparation time: 5 minutes
Cooking time: 33 minutes
Servings: 6

Ingredients:

Grouper:

2 lb Grouper, cut into 3 pieces each
1 tsp Cumin Powder
½ tsp Garlic Powder
½ tsp Onion Powder
½ tsp Coriander Powder
¼ cup Fish Seasoning
¼ cup Pecan Oil
Salt to taste
White Pepper to taste

Beurre Blanc:

1 lb Butter
2 tbsp Apple Cider Vinegar
2 Shallots, minced
1 tsp Peppercorns, crushed
5 oz Heavy Cream,
Salt to taste
2 sprigs Dill
1 tbsp Lemon juice
1 tbsp Saffron Powder

Instructions:

1. Make a water bath, place Sous Vide cooker in it, and set it at 132 F.
2. Season the grouper pieces with salt and white pepper.
3. Place them in a vacuum-sealable bag, release air by the water displacement method, seal and submerge the bag in the water bath.
4. Set the timer for 30 minutes.
5. Mix the cumin, garlic, onion, coriander, and fish seasoning. Place aside.
6. Meanwhile, make the beurre nantais by placing a pan over medium heat and adding, shallots, vinegar, and peppercorns. Cook to attain a syrup.
7. Reduce heat to low and add butter, whisking continuously.
8. Add dill, lemon juice, and saffron powder, stir continuously and cook for 2 minutes.
9. Add cream and season with salt. Cook for 1 minute.
10. Turn heat off and place aside.
11. Once the Sous Vide timer has stopped, remove and unseal the bag.
12. Set a skillet over medium heat, add pecan oil.
13. Pat dry the grouper and seasoning with the spice mixture and sear them in the heated oil.
14. Serve grouper and beurre nantais with a side of steamed spinach.

Nutrition facts per serving: Calories 326, Total Fat 46g, Sodium 2,329mg, Potassium 1324mg, Total Carbs 3g, Net Carbs 3g, Protein 75g

Tuna with Ginger Sauce

Preparation time: 10 minutes
Cooking time: 32 minutes
Servings: 6

Ingredients:

Tuna:

3 Tuna Steaks

Salt to taste

Black Pepper to taste

⅓ cup Olive Oil

2 tbsp Canola Oil

½ cup Black Sesame Seeds

½ cup White Sesame Seeds

Ginger Sauce:

1 inch Ginger, grated

2 Shallots, minced

1 Red Chili, minced

3 tbsp Water

2 ½ Lime Juice

1 ½ tbsp Rice Vinegar

2 ½ tbsp Soy Sauce

1 tbsp Fish Sauce

1 ½ tbsp Sugar

1 bunch Green Lettuce Leaves

Instructions:

1. Start with the sauce: place a small pan over low heat and add olive oil.

2. Once it has heated, add ginger and chili. Cook for 3 minutes

3. Add sugar and vinegar, stir and cook until the sugar dissolves.

4. Pour water and bring to a boil.

5. Add the soy sauce, fish sauce, and lime juice and cook for 2 minutes.

6. Set aside to cool.

7. Make a water bath, place a Sous Vide cooker in it, and set it at 110 F.

8. Season the tuna with salt and pepper and place in 3 separate vacuum-sealable bags.

9. Add olive oil, release air from the bag by the water displacement method, seal and submerge the bag in the water bath.

10. Set the timer for 30 minutes.

11. Once the timer has stopped, remove and unseal the bag. Set the tuna aside.

12. Place a skillet over low heat and add canola oil.

13. While heating, mix sesame seeds in a bowl.

14. Pat dry tuna, coat them in sesame seeds and sear top and bottom in heated oil until seeds start to toast. Slice tuna into thin strips.

15. Layer a serving platter with lettuce and arrange tuna on the bed of lettuce.

16. Serve with ginger sauce as a starter.

Nutrition facts per serving: Calories 184, Total Fat 6g, Sodium 50mg, Potassium 323mg, Total Carbs 11g, Net Carbs 8g, Protein 30g

Basil Halibut

Preparation time: 3 minutes
Cooking time: 40 minutes
Servings: 2

Ingredients:

2 lb Halibut Filets

3 sprigs Basil Leaves

1 tsp Garlic Powder

1 tsp Onion Powder

½ tsp Salt

1 tsp White Pepper

2 ½ tsp + 2 tsp Butter

2 Shallots, peeled and halved

2 sprigs Thyme

Lemon wedges for garnishing

Instructions:

1. Make a water bath, place a Sous Vide cooker in it, and set it at 124 F.
2. Cut halibut filets into 3 pieces each and rub with salt, garlic powder, onion powder, and pepper.
3. Place the filets, basil, and 2 ½ teaspoons of butter into 3 different vacuum-sealable bags.
4. Release air by the water displacement method and seal the bags. Place them in the water bath and cook for 40 minutes.
5. Once the timer has stopped, remove and unseal the bag. Place a skillet over low heat and add the remaining butter.
6. Once it is heated, remove the skin of the halibuts and pat dry. Add halibuts with shallots and thyme and sear bottom and top until crispy. Garnish with lemon wedges. Serve with a side of steamed vegetables.

Nutrition facts per serving: Calories 186, Total Fat 14g, Sodium 80mg, Potassium 268mg, Total Carbs 0g, Net Carbs 0g, Protein 14g

Parsley Prawns

Preparation time: 20 minutes
Cooking time: 10 minutes
Servings: 4

Ingredients:

12 large Prawns, peeled and deveined

1 tsp Salt

1 tsp Sugar

3 tsp Olive Oil

1 Bay Leaf

1 sprig Parsley, chopped

2 tbsp Lemon Zest

1 tbsp Lemon Juice

Instructions:

1. Make a water bath, place a Sous Vide cooker in it, and set at 156 F.
2. Add prawns to a bowl, add salt and sugar, mix and let it sit for 15 minutes. Rinse the prawns with water.
3. Place the prawns, bay leaf, olive oil, and lemon zest in a vacuum-sealable bag. Release air by the water displacement method and seal it.
4. Submerge prawns in the water bath and set the timer for 10 minutes.
5. Once the timer has stopped, remove and unseal the bag.
6. Dish prawns and drizzle with lemon juice. Serve as a starter.

Nutrition facts per serving: Calories 120, Total Fat 1g, Sodium 440mg, Total Carbs 0.1g, Net Carbs 0.1g, Protein 7g

Delicious Buttered Scallops

Preparation time: 15 minutes
Cooking time: 40 minutes
Servings: 3

Ingredients:

½ lb Scallops
3 tsp Butter (2 tsp for cooking + 1 tsp for searing)
Salt to taste
Pepper to taste

Instructions:

1. Make a water bath, place a Sous Vide machine in it, and set it at 140 F.
2. Pat dry scallops using a napkin.
3. Place scallops, salt, 2 tablespoons of butter, and pepper in a vacuum-sealable bag.
4. Release air by the water displacement method, seal and submerge the bag in the water bath and set the timer for 40 minutes.
5. Once the timer has stopped, remove and unseal the bag.
6. Pat dry the scallops using a napkin and place aside.
7. Set a skillet over medium heat and the remaining butter.
8. Once it has melted, sear the scallops on both sides until golden brown.
9. Serve with a side of buttered mixed vegetables.

Nutrition facts per serving: Calories 111, Total Fat 0.8g, Sodium 667mg, Potassium 314mg, Total Carbs 5g, Net Carbs 4.9, Protein 21g

Oregano Octopus Grill

Preparation time: 20 minutes

Cooking time: 5 hours 15 minutes

Servings: 3

Ingredients:

½ lb medium Octopus Tentacles, blanched

3 tbsp Salt

3 tbsp Black Pepper

3 tsp + 3 tbsp Olive Oil

2 tsp dried Oregano

2 sprigs fresh Parsley, chopped

Ice for an ice bath

Instructions:

1. Make a water bath, place a Sous Vide cooker in it, and set it at 171 F.
2. Place octopus, salt, 3 teaspoons of olive oil, and pepper in a vacuum-sealable bag. Release air by the water displacement method, seal and submerge the bag in the water bath. Set the timer for 5 hours.
3. Once the timer has stopped, remove the bag and cover it in the ice bath. Place aside to cool octopus completely. Preheat a grill.
4. Once the grill is hot, transfer the octopus to a plate, add 3 tablespoons of olive oil and massage. Grill octopus to char nicely on each side.
5. Dish octopus and garnish with parsley and oregano. Serve with a sweet, spicy dip.

Nutrition facts per serving: Calories 603, Total Fat 34g, Potassium 372mg, Total Carbs 1.1g, Net Carbs 1.1g, Protein 32g

Rosemary Tuna Flakes

Preparation time: 15 minutes
Cooking time: 1 hour 30 minutes
Servings: 4

Ingredients:

¼ lb Tuna Steak

1 tsp Rosemary Leaves

1 tsp Thyme Leaves

2 cups Olive Oil

1 clove Garlic, minced

Instructions:

1. Make a water bath, place a Sous Vide cooker in it, and set it at 135 °F.
2. Place the tuna steak, salt, rosemary, garlic, thyme, and two tablespoons of oil in the vacuum-sealable bag.
3. Release air by the water displacement method, seal and submerge the bag in the water bath. Set the timer for 1 hour 30 minutes.
4. Once the timer has stopped, remove and unseal the bag.
5. Place the tuna in a bowl and set it aside. Place a skillet over high heat, add the remaining olive oil. Once it has heated, pour it over the tuna.
6. Flake the tuna using two forks. Transfer and store in an airtight container with olive oil for up to a week. Serve in salads.

Nutrition facts per serving: Calories 90, Total Fat 5g, Sodium 280mg, Total Carbs 1g, Net Carbs 1g, Protein 9g

VEGETABLES

Snow Peas with Mint

Preparation time: 10 minutes
Cooking time: 15 minutes
Servings: 2

Ingredients:

1 tbsp Butter
½ cup Snow Peas
1 tbsp Mint Leaves, chopped
A pinch Salt
Sugar to taste

Instructions:

1. Make a water bath, place a Sous Vide cooker in it, and set it at 183 F.
2. Place all the ingredients in a vacuum-sealable bag.
3. Release air by the water displacement method, seal the bag and submerge in the water bath.
4. Set the timer for 15 minutes.
5. Once the timer has stopped, remove and unseal the bag.
6. Transfer the ingredients to a serving plate. Serve as a condiment.

Nutrition facts per serving: Calories 117, Total Fat 0.6g, Sodium 7mg, Potassium 354mg, Protein 8g, Total Carbs 8.1g, Net Carbs 6.3

Herbed Asparagus Mix

Preparation time: 15 minutes
Cooking time: 12 minutes
Servings: 3

Ingredients:

1 ½ lb medium Asparagus

5 tbsp Butter

2 tbsp Lemon Juice

½ tsp Lemon Zest

1 tbsp Chives, sliced

1 tbsp Parsley, chopped

1 tbsp + 1 tbsp Fresh Dill, chopped

1 tbsp + 1 tbsp Tarragon, chopped

Instructions:

1. Make a water bath, place the Sous Vide cooker in it, and set to 183 °F. Cut off and discard the tight bottoms of the asparagus. Place the asparagus in a vacuum-sealable bag.

2. Release air by the water displacement method, seal and submerge the bag in the water bath and set the timer for 10 minutes.

3. Once the timer has stopped, remove the bag and unseal it. Place a skillet over low heat, add the butter and steamed asparagus. Season with salt and pepper and toss continually. Add lemon juice and zest and cook for 2 minutes.

4. Turn heat off and add parsley, 1 tablespoon of dill, and 1 tablespoon of tarragon. Toss evenly. Garnish with remaining dill and tarragon. Serve warm as a side dish.

Nutrition facts per serving: Calories 190, Total Fat 0.1g, Sodium 2mg, Potassium 202mg, Total Carbohydrate 3.9g, Net Carbs 1.8g, Protein 2.2g

Balsamic Braised Cabbage

Preparation time: 15 minutes
Cooking time: 1 hour 30 minutes
Servings: 3

Ingredients:

1 lb Red Cabbage, quartered and core removed
1 Shallot, thinly sliced
2 cloves Garlic, thinly sliced
½ tbsp Balsamic Vinegar
½ tbsp Unsalted Butter
Salt to taste

Instructions:

1. Make a water bath, place Sous Vide cooker in it, and set to 185 F.
2. Divide cabbage and remaining ingredients into 2 vacuum-sealable bags.
3. Release air by the water displacement method and seal the bags.
4. Submerge them in the water bath and set the timer to cook for 1 hour 30 minutes.
5. Once the timer has stopped, remove and unseal the bag.
6. Transfer the cabbage with juices into serving plates.
7. Season with salt and vinegar to taste.
8. Serve as a side dish.

Nutrition facts per serving: Calories 129, Total Fat 6g, Total Carbs 3g, Net Carbs 1g, Sodium 116mg, Protein 2g

Nuts, Beetroot & Cheese Salad

Preparation time: 15 minutes

Cooking time: 2 hours 30 seconds

Servings: 3

Ingredients:

1 lb Beetroot, peeled

½ cup Almonds, blanched

2 tbsp Hazelnuts, skinned

2 tsp Olive Oil

1 clove Garlic, finely minced

1 tsp Cumin Powder

1 tsp Lemon Zest

Salt to taste

½ cup Goat Cheese, crumbled

Fresh Mint Leaves to garnish

Dressing:

2 tbsp Olive Oil

1 tbsp Apple Cider Vinegar

Instructions:

1. Make a water bath, place the Sous Vide cooker in it, and set at 183 F.
2. Cut the beetroots into wedges and bag in a vacuum-sealable bag.
3. Release air by the water displacement method, seal and submerge the bag in the water bath and set the timer for 2 hours. Once the timer has stopped, remove and unseal the bag. Place the beetroot aside.
4. Put a pan over medium heat, add almonds and hazelnuts, and toast for 3 minutes. Transfer to a cutting board and chop.
5. Add oil to the same pan, add garlic and cumin. Cook for 30 seconds. Turn heat off. In a bowl, combine the goat cheese, almond mixture, lemon zest and garlic mixture. Mix. Whisk olive oil and vinegar and place aside. Serve as a side dish.

Nutrition facts per serving: Calories 127, Total Fat 7g, Total Carbs 2.7g, Net Carbs 0.47g, Sodium 305mg, Potassium 404mg, Protein 7g

Creamy Cauliflower Broccoli Soup

Preparation time: 5 minutes
Cooking time: 2 hours 3 minutes
Servings: 2

Ingredients:

1 medium Cauliflower, cut into small florets
½ lb Broccoli, cut into small florets
1 Green Bell Pepper, chopped
1 medium White Onion, diced
1 tsp Olive Oil
1 clove Garlic, crushed
½ cup Vegetable Stock
½ cup of Skimmed Milk

Instructions:

1. Make a water bath, place the Sous Vide machine in it, and set it to 185 °F.
2. Place the cauliflower, broccoli, bell pepper, and white onion in a vacuum-sealable bag and pour olive oil into it.
3. Release air by the water displacement method and seal the bag. Submerge the bag in the water bath. Set the timer for 50 minutes and cook.
4. Once the timer has stopped, remove the bag and unseal it. Transfer the vegetables to a blender, add garlic and milk, and puree to smooth.
5. Place a pan over medium heat, add the vegetable puree and vegetable stock and simmer for 3 minutes. Season with salt and pepper. Serve warm as a side dish.

Nutrition facts per serving: Calories 102, Total Fat 5.9g, Sodium 212mg, Potassium 255mg, Total Carbs 5g, Net Carbs 3g, Protein 3g

Mediterranean Eggplant Lasagna

Preparation time: 20 minutes
Cooking time: 2 hours
Servings: 3

Ingredients:

1 lb Eggplant, peeled and thinly sliced
1 tsp Salt
1 cup Tomato Sauce, divided into 3
2 oz Fresh Mozzarella, thinly sliced
1 oz Parmesan Cheese, grated
2 oz Italian Blend Cheese, grated
3 tbsp Fresh Basil, chopped

Topping:

½ tbsp Macadamia Nuts, toasted and chopped
1 oz Parmesan Cheese, grated
1 oz Italian Blend Cheese, grated

Instructions:

1. Make a water bath, place Sous Vide cooker in it, and set at 183 F.
2. Place eggplants in a colander, toss with salt and let drain for 15 minutes.
3. While water heats, peel eggplants, slice into thin rounds and toss with salt.
4. Lay a vacuum-sealable bag on its side, make a layer of half the eggplant, spread one portion of tomato sauce, layer mozzarella, then parmesan, then cheese blend, then basil.
5. Top with the second portion of tomato sauce.
6. Seal the bag carefully by the water displacement method, keeping it flat as possible.

7. Submerge the bag flat in the water bath.

8. Set the timer for 2 hours and cook.

9. Release air 2 to 3 times within the first 30 minutes as eggplant releases gas as it cooks.

10. Once the timer has stopped, remove the bag gently and poke one corner of the bag using a pin to release liquid from the bag.

11. Lay the bag flat on a serving plate, cut open the top of it and gently slide the lasagna onto the plate.

12. Top with remaining tomato sauce, macadamia nuts, cheese blend, and Parmesan cheese.

13. Melt and brown the cheese using a torch.

Nutrition facts per serving: Calories 25, Total Fat 0.2g, Potassium 229mg, Total Carbs 6g, Net Carbs 3g, Protein 1g

Traditional Ratatouille

Preparation time: 30 minutes
Cooking time: 1 hour 50 minutes
Servings: 3

Ingredients:

2 medium Zucchini, cut into ¼ inch dices
2 medium Tomatoes, cut into ¼ inch dices
2 Red Capsicum, seeded and cut into 2-inch dices
1 small Eggplant, cut into ¼ inch dices
1 Onion, cut into 1-inch dices
Salt to taste
½ Red Pepper Flakes
8 cloves Garlic, crushed
2 ½ tbsp Olive Oil
5 sprigs + 2 sprigs Basil Leaves

Instructions:

1. Make a water bath, place a Sous Vide cooker in it, and set it at 185 F.
2. Place the tomatoes, zucchini, onion, bell pepper and eggplant each in 5 separate vacuum-sealable bags.
3. Put garlic, basil leaves, and 1 tablespoon of olive oil in each bag.
4. Release air by the water displacement method, seal and submerge the bags in the water bath and set the timer for 20 minutes.
5. Once the timer has stopped, remove the bag with the tomatoes.
6. Place aside.
7. Reset the timer for 30 minutes.

8. Once the timer has stopped, remove the bags with the zucchinis and red bell peppers. Place aside.

9. Reset the timer for 1 hour.

10. Once the timer has stopped, remove the remaining bags and discard the garlic and basil leaves.

11. In a bowl, add tomatoes and use a spoon to mash them lightly.

12. Roughly chop the remaining vegetables and add to the tomatoes.

13. Season with salt, red pepper flakes, remaining olive oil, and basil.

14. Serve as a side dish.

Nutrition facts per serving: Calories 200, Protein 20g, Total Fat 3g, Total Carbs 8.1g, Net Carbs 6.9g, Sodium 90mg, Protein 1.69g

Speedy Poached Tomatoes

Preparation time: 5 minutes
Cooking time: 30 minutes
Servings: 3

Ingredients:

4 cups Cherry Tomatoes
5 tbsp Olive Oil
½ tbsp Fresh Rosemary Leaves, minced
½ tbsp Fresh Thyme Leaves, minced
Salt to taste
Pepper to taste

Instructions:

1. Make a water bath, place Sous Vide machine in it, and set to 131 °F.
2. Divide the listed ingredients into 2 vacuum-sealable bags, season with salt and pepper.
3. Release air by the water displacement method and seal the bags.
4. Submerge them in the water bath and set the timer to cook for 30 minutes.
5. Once the timer has stopped, remove the bag and unseal it.
6. Transfer the tomatoes with the juices into a bowl. Serve as a side dish.

Nutrition facts per serving: Calories 180, Sodium 95mg, Total Fat 16g, Total Carbs 5g, Net Carbs 4g, Protein 34g

Chili Brussels Sprouts in Sweet Syrup

Preparation time: 20 minutes

Cooking time: 56 minutes

Servings: 3

Ingredients:

4 lb Brussels Sprouts, stems trimmed and halved

3 tbsp Olive Oil

¾ cup Fish Sauce

3 tbsp Water

2 tbsp Sugar

1 ½ tbsp Rice Vinegar

2 tsp Lime Juice

3 Red Chilies, sliced thinly

2 cloves Garlic, minced

Instructions:

1. Make a water bath, place a Sous Vide cooker in it, and set it at 183 F.

2. Pour Brussels sprouts, salt, and oil in a vacuum-sealable bag, release air by the water displacement method, seal and submerge the bag in the water bath. Set the timer for 50 minutes.

3. Once the timer has stopped, remove the bag, unseal it, and transfer the Brussels sprouts to a foiled baking sheet.

4. Preheat a broiler to high, place the baking sheet in it, and broil for 6 minutes. Pour the Brussels sprouts in a bowl.

5. Make the sauce: in a bowl, add the remaining listed cooking ingredients and stir. Add the sauce to the Brussels sprouts and toss evenly. Serve as a side dish.

Nutrition facts per serving: Calories 43, Total Fat 0.3g, Sodium 25mg, Potassium 389mg, Total Carbs 9g, Net Carbs 5.2g, Protein 3.4g

Aromatic Braised Beetroots

Preparation time: 15 minutes
Cooking time: 1 hour
Servings: 3

Ingredients:

2 Beets, peeled and sliced into 1 cm inches
⅓ cup Balsamic Vinegar
½ tsp Olive Oil
⅓ cup Toasted Walnuts
⅓ cup Grana Padano Cheese, grated
Salt to taste
Pepper to taste

Instructions:

1. Make a water bath, place a Sous Vide cooker in it, and set it at 183 °F.
2. Place the beets, vinegar, and salt in a vacuum-sealable bag.
3. Release air by the water displacement method, seal and submerge the bag in the water bath. Set the timer for 1 hour.
4. Once the timer has stopped, remove and unseal the bag.
5. Transfer the beets to a bowl, add olive oil and toss.
6. Sprinkle walnuts and cheese over it.
7. Serve as a side dish.

Nutrition facts per serving: Calories 43, Total Fat 0.3g, Sodium 79mg, Potassium 326mg, Total Carbs 10g, Net Carbs 7.1g, Protein 1.7g

Pomodoro Soup

Preparation time: 10 minutes
Cooking time: 50 minutes
Servings: 3

Ingredients:

2 lb Tomatoes, halved

1 Onion, diced

1 Celery Stick, chopped

3 tbsp Olive Oil

1 tbsp unsweetened Tomato Puree

A pinch of Sugar

1 Bay Leaf

Instructions:

1. Make a water bath, place a Sous Vide cooker in it, and set it at 185 F.
2. Place all the listed ingredients except salt in bowl and toss. Put them in a vacuum-sealable bag.
3. Release air by the water displacement method, seal and submerge the bag into the water bath. Set the timer for 40 minutes.
4. Once the timer has stopped, remove the bag and unseal it.
5. Puree the ingredients using a blender.
6. Pour the blended tomato into a pot and set it over medium heat. Season with salt and cook for 10 minutes. Dish soup into bowls and cool.

Nutrition facts per serving: Calories 270, Total Fat 4g, Total Carbs 3.2g, Net Carbs 2.7g, Sodium 810mg, Protein 18g

Simple Mushroom Soup

Preparation time: 4 minutes
Cooking time: 40 minutes
Servings: 3

Ingredients:

1 lb Mixed Mushrooms

2 Onions, diced

3 cloves Garlic

2 sprigs Parsley Leaves, chopped

2 tbsp Thyme Powder

2 tbsp Olive Oil

2 cups Cream

2 cups Vegetable Stock (see recipe above)

Instructions:

1. Make a water bath, place a Sous Vide cooker in it, and set it at 185 F.
2. Place the mushrooms, onion, and celery in a vacuum-sealable bag.
3. Release air by the water displacement method, seal and submerge the bag in the water bath. Set the timer for 30 minutes. Once the timer has stopped, remove and unseal the bag.
4. Blend the ingredients in the bag in a blender. Put a pan over medium heat, add the olive oil. Once it starts to heat, add the pureed mushrooms and the remaining listed ingredients except for the cream. Cook for 10 minutes.
5. Turn off heat and add cream. Stir well. Serve with a side of bread.

Nutrition facts per serving: Calories 22, Total Fat 0.3g, Sodium 5mg, Potassium 318mg, Total Carbs 4.2g, Net Carbs 3.2g, Protein 3.1g

Easy Mixed Vegetable Soup

Preparation time: 10 minutes

Cooking time: 40 minutes

Servings: 3

Ingredients:

1 Sweet Onion, sliced

1 tsp Garlic Powder

2 cups Zucchini, cut in small dices

3 oz Parmesan Rind

2 cups Baby Spinach

2 tbsp Olive Oil

1 tsp Red Pepper Flakes

2 cups Vegetable Stock

1 sprig Rosemary

Salt to taste

Instructions:

1. Make a water bath, place a Sous Vide cooker in it, and set it at 185 F.

2. Toss all the ingredients with olive oil except the garlic and salt, and place them in a vacuum-sealable bag.

3. Release air by water displacement method, seal and submerge the bag in the water bath. Set the timer for 30 minutes.

4. Once the timer has stopped, remove and unseal the bag. Discard the rosemary. Pour the remaining ingredients into a pot and add the salt and garlic powder.

5. Once the timer has stopped, remove and unseal the bag. Discard the rosemary. Pour the remaining ingredients into a pot and add the salt and garlic powder.

6. Put the pot over medium heat and simmer for 10 minutes. Serve as a light dish.

Nutrition facts per serving: Calories 150, Total Fat 0.3g, Sodium 101mg, Total Carbs 15g, Net Carbs 8g, Protein 1.2g

Power Green Soup

Preparation time: 10 minutes
Cooking time: 40 minutes
Servings: 3

Ingredients:

4 cups Vegetable Stock
1 tbsp Olive Oil
1 clove Garlic, crushed
1-inch Ginger, sliced
1 tsp Coriander Powder
1 large Zucchini, diced
3 cups Kale
2 cups Broccoli, cut into florets
1 Lime, juiced and zested

Instructions:

1. Make a water bath, place a Sous Vide cooker in it, and set it at 185 °F.
2. Place the broccoli, zucchini, kale, and parsley in a vacuum-sealable bag.
3. Release air by the water displacement method, seal and submerge the bag in the water bath. Set the timer for 30 minutes.
4. Once the timer has stopped, remove and unseal the bagAdd the steamed ingredients to a blender with garlic and ginger. Puree to smooth.
5. Pour the green puree into a pot and add the remaining listed ingredients.
6. Put the pot over medium heat and simmer for 10 minutes. Serve as a light dish.

Nutrition facts per serving: Calories 153, Sodium 184mg, Total Fat 1g, Total Carbs 3.2g, Net Carbs 0.8g, Protein 6g

Simple Hard-Boiled Eggs

Preparation time: 10 minutes

Cooking time: 1 hour

Servings: 6

Ingredients:

6 large Eggs

Ice bath

Instructions:

1. Make a water bath, place a Sous Vide cooker in it, and set it at 165 °F.
2. Place the eggs in the water bath and set the timer for 1 hour.
3. Once the timer has stopped, transfer the eggs to the ice bath.
4. Peel eggs. Serve as a snack or in salads.

Nutrition facts per serving: Calories 78, Total Fat 5.3g, Sodium 70mg, Potassium 63mg, Protein 6.3g, Total Carbs 0g, Net Carbs 0g

Colorful Bell Pepper Mix

Preparation time: 20 minutes
Cooking time: 15 minutes
Servings: 2

Ingredients:

1 Red Bell Pepper, chopped
1 Yellow Bell Pepper, chopped
1 Green Bell Pepper, chopped
1 Large Orange Bell Pepper, chopped
Salt to taste

Instructions:

1. Make a water bath, place a Sous Vide cooker in it, and set it at 183 F.
2. Place all the bell peppers with salt in a vacuum-sealable bag.
3. Release air by the water displacement method, seal and submerge in the water bath.
4. Set the timer for 15 minutes.
5. Once the timer has stopped, remove and unseal the bag.
6. Serve bell peppers with its juices as a side dish.

Nutrition facts per serving: Calories 31, Total Fat 0.4g, Sodium 2mg, Potassium 251mg, Protein 1g, Total Carbs 7g, Net Carbs 4.8g

Cilantro Curried Zucchinis

Preparation time: 10 minutes
Cooking time: 25 minutes
Servings: 3

Ingredients:

3 small Zucchinis, diced

2 tsp Curry Powder

1 tbsp Olive Oil

Salt to taste

Pepper to taste

¼ cup Cilantro

Instructions:

1. Make a water bath, place a Sous Vide cooker in it, and set it at 185 °F.
2. Place the zucchinis in a vacuum-sealable bag.
3. Release air by the water displacement method, seal and submerge the bag in the water bath. Set the timer for 20 minutes.
4. Once the timer has stopped, remove and unseal the bag.
5. Place a skillet over medium, add olive oil.
6. Once it has heated, add the zucchinis and the remaining listed ingredients.
7. Season with salt and stir-fry for 5 minutes.
8. Serve as a side dish.

Nutrition facts per serving: Calories 17, Total Fat 0.3g, Sodium 8mg, Potassium 261mg, Total Carbs 3.1g, Net Carbs 2.1g, Protein 1.2g

STOCKS & BROTHS

Classic Beef Broth

Preparation time: 3 minutes
Cooking time: 14 hours 15 minutes
Servings: 6

Ingredients:

3 lb Beef Feet
1 ½ lb Beef Bones
½ lb Grounded Beef
5 cups Tomato Paste, unsweetened
6 medium Sweet Onions
3 heads Garlic
6 tbsp Black Pepper Powder
5 sprigs Thyme
4 Bay Leaves
10 cups Water

Instructions:

1. Preheat an oven to 425 °F.
2. Place beef bones and beef feet in a roasting pan and rub them with the
3. tomato paste. Add garlic and onion. Place aside.
4. Place and crumble ground beef in another roasting pan.
5. Place the roasting pans in the oven and roast until dark brown.
6. Once done, drain fat from the roasting pans.

7. Make a water bath in a large container, place a Sous Vide cooker in it, and set it at 195 F.

8. Separate the ground beef, roasted vegetables, black pepper, thyme, and bay leaves in 3 vacuum bags.

9. Deglaze the roasting pans with water and add it to the bags.

10. Fold the top of the bags 2 to 3 times.

11. Place the bags in the water bath and clip it to the Sous Vide container.

12. Set the timer for 13 hours.

13. Once the timer has stopped, remove the bags and transfer the ingredients to a pot.

14. Bring the ingredients to a boil over high heat.

15. Cook for 15 minutes.

16. Turn off heat and strain.

17. Use the stock as a soup base.

Nutrition facts per serving: Calories 31, Total Fat 0.2g, Sodium 475mg, Potassium 444mg, Total Carbs 4.1g, Net Carbs 2.9g, Protein 4.78g

Homemade Chicken Stock

Preparation time: 20 minutes
Cooking time: 12 hours 10 minutes
Servings: 3

Ingredients:

2 lb Chicken, any parts – thighs, breasts
5 cups Water
2 Celery Sticks, chopped
2 White Onions, chopped

Instructions:

1. Make a water bath, place a Sous Vide cooker in it, and set it at 194 F.
2. Separate the listed ingredients in 2 vacuum bags, fold the top of the bags 2 – 3 times.
3. Place them in the water bath and clip it to the Sous Vide container.
4. Set the timer for 12 hours.
5. Once the timer has stopped, remove the bag and transfer the ingredients to a pot.
6. Boil the ingredients over high heat for 10 minutes.
7. Turn off heat and strain. Use the stock as a soup base.

Nutrition facts per serving: Calories 86, Total Fat 2.9g, Cholesterol 7mg, Sodium 343mg, Potassium 252mg, Total Carbs 4.5g, Net Carbs 4.5g, Protein 6.1g

Kombu Fish Broth

Preparation time: 10 minutes
Cooking time: 10 hours 5 minutes
Servings: 4

Ingredients:

5 cups Water
½ lb Fish fillets, skin
1 lb Fish Head
5 medium Green Onions
3 Sweet Onion
¼ lb Black Seaweed (Kombu)

Instructions:

1. Make a water bath, place a Sous Vide cooker in it, and set it at 194 F.
2. Separate all the listed ingredients equally into 2 vacuum bags, fold the top of the bags 2 times.
3. Place them in the water bath and clip it to the Sous Vide container. Set the timer for 10 hours.
4. Once the timer has stopped, remove the bag and transfer the ingredients to a pot.
5. Boil the ingredients over high heat for 5 minutes
6. Turn off heat and strain.
7. Refrigerate and use for up to 14 days.

Nutrition facts per serving: Calories 39, Total Fat 1.5g, Sodium 776mg, Potassium 210mg, Total Carbs 1.5g, Net Carbs 1.1g, Protein 22g

Rosemary Seafood Stock

Preparation time: 10 minutes
Cooking time: 10 hours
Servings: 6

Ingredients:

1 lb Shrimp Shells, with heads and tails
3 cups Water
1 tbsp Olive Oil
2 tsp Salt
2 sprigs Rosemary
½ head Garlic, crushed
½ cup Celery Leaves, chopped

Instructions:

1. Make a water bath, place a Sous Vide cooker in it, and set it at 180 F.
2. Toss the shrimp with the olive oil. Place the shrimp with the remaining listed ingredients in a vacuum-sealable bag.
3. Release air, seal and submerge the bag into the water bath, and set the timer for 10 hours.
4. Once the timer has stopped, remove and unseal the bag. Strain the ingredients. Cool and use frozen for up to 2 weeks.

Nutrition facts per serving: Calories 10, Sodium 480mg, Potassium 80mg, Total Carbs 0g, Net Carbs 0g, Protein 2g

Basic Vegetable Stock

Preparation time: 15 minutes
Cooking time: 12 hours 20 minutes
Servings: 10

Ingredients:

1 ½ cups Celery Root, diced

1 ½ cups Leeks, diced

½ cup Fennel, diced

4 cloves Garlic, crushed

1 tbsp Olive Oil

6 cups Water

1 ½ cups Mushrooms

½ cup Parsley, chopped

1 tbsp Black Peppercorns

1 Bay Leaf

Instructions:

1. Make a water bath, place a Sous Vide cooker in it, and set it at 180 °F. Preheat an oven to 450 F. Place the leeks, celery, fennel, garlic, and olive oil in a bowl. Toss them. Transfer to a roasting pan and tuck them in the oven. Roast for 20 minutes.

2. Place the roasted vegetables with its juices, water, parsley, peppercorns, mushrooms, and bay leaf in a vacuum-sealable bag.

3. Release air, seal and submerge the bag into the water bath and set the timer for 12 hours.

4. Cover the water bath's container with a plastic wrap to reduce evaporation and keep adding water to the bath to keep the vegetables covered.

5. Once the timer has stopped, remove and unseal the bag. Strain the ingredients. Cool and use frozen for up to 1 month.

Nutrition facts per serving: Calories 15, Total Fat 0g, Sodium 570mg, Total Carbs 3g, Net Carbs 3g, Protein 0g

SAUCES, SPICES & DIPS

Paprika Bell Pepper Puree

Preparation time: 20 minutes
Cooking time: 23 minutes
Servings: 4

Ingredients:

8 Red Bell Peppers, cored
⅓ cup Olive Oil
2 tbsp Lemon Juice
3 cloves Garlic, crushed
2 tsp Sweet Paprika

Instructions:

1. Make a water bath and place a Sous Vide cooker in it and set it at 183 F.
2. Put the bell peppers, garlic, and olive oil in a vacuum-sealable bag.
3. Release air by the water displacement method, seal and submerge the bags in the water bath. Set the timer for 20 minutes and cook.
4. Once the timer has stopped, remove the bag and unseal it. Transfer the bell pepper and garlic to a blender and puree to smooth.
5. Place a pan over medium heat; add bell pepper puree and the remaining listed ingredients. Cook for 3 minutes. Serve warm or cold as a dip.

Nutrition facts per serving: Calories 20, Total Fat 0.2g, Sodium 3mg, Potassium 175mg, Total Carbs 7.1g, Net Carbs 4.8g, Protein 0.9g

Artichoke Hearts with Green Chilies

Preparation time: 1 hour 15 minutes

Cooking time: 33 minutes

Servings: 6

Ingredients:

2 tbsp Butter

2 Onions, quartered

3 cloves Garlic, minced

15 oz Artichoke Hearts, soaked for 1 hour, drained and chopped

18 oz Frozen Spinach, thawed

5 oz Green Chilies

3 tbsp Olive Oil Mayonnaise

3 tbsp Whipped Cream Cheese

Instructions:

1. Make a water bath, place a Sous Vide cooker in it, and set it at 181 F. Divide the onions, garlic, artichoke hearts, spinach, and green chilies into 2 vacuum-sealable bags.

2. Release air by the water displacement method, seal and submerge the bags in the water bath. Set the timer for 30 minutes to cook.

3. Once the timer has stopped, remove and unseal the bag. Puree the ingredients using a blender. Place a pan over medium heat and add the butter.

4. Once it has melted, add the vegetable puree, lemon juice, olive oil mayonnaise, and cream cheese. Season with salt and pepper. Stir and cook for 3 minutes. Serve warm with a side of vegetable strips.

Nutrition facts per serving: Calories 47, Total Fat 0.2g, Sodium 94mg, Potassium 370mg, Total Carbs 2g, Net Carbs 2g, Protein 3.3g

Homemade Spicy BBQ Sauce

Preparation time: 10 minutes

Cooking time: 1 hour

Servings: 10

Ingredients:

1 ½ lb small Tomatoes

¼ cup Apple Cider Vinegar

¼ tsp Sugar

1 tbsp Worcestershire Sauce

½ tbsp Liquid Hickory Smoke

2 tsp Smoked Paprika

2 tsp Garlic Powder

1 tsp Onion Powder

Salt to taste

½ tsp Chili Powder

½ tsp Cayenne pepper

4 tbsp Water

Instructions:

1. Make a water bath, place a Sous Vide cooker in it, and set it at 185 F.
2. Separate the tomatoes into two vacuum-sealable bags.
3. Release air by the water displacement method, seal and submerge the bags in the water bath. Set the timer for 40 minutes.
4. Once the timer has stopped, remove and unseal the bag.
5. Transfer the tomatoes to a blender and puree until smooth and thick. Do not add water.
6. Put a pot over medium heat, add the tomato puree and the remaining listed ingredients. Bring to a boil, stirring continuously for 20 minutes. A thick consistency should be achieved.
7. Use as a sauce for barbecuing.

Nutrition facts per serving: Calories 22, Total Fat 0.9g, Sodium 7mg, Potassium 245mg, Total Carbs 4.5g, Net Carbs 4.5g, Protein 1.2g

Basil Tomato Sauce

Preparation time: 20 minutes
Cooking time: 40 minutes
Servings: 4

Ingredients:

1 (16 oz) can Tomatoes, crushed

1 small White Onion, diced

1 cup fresh Basil Leaves

1 tbsp Olive Oil

1 clove Garlic, crushed

Salt to taste

1 Bay Leaf

1 Red Chili

Instructions:

1. Make a water bath, place a Sous Vide cooker in it, and set it at 185 °F.
2. Place all the listed ingredients in a vacuum-sealable bag.
3. Release air by the water displacement method, seal and submerge the bag in the water bath. Set the timer for 40 minutes. Once the timer has stopped, remove and unseal the bag.
4. Discard the bay leaf and transfer the remaining ingredients to a blender and puree smooth. Serve as a side sauce.

Nutrition facts per serving: Calories 18, Total Fat 0.2g, Sodium 5mg, Potassium 237mg, Total Carbs 3.9g, Net Carbs 3.2g, Protein 0.9g

Fresh Ginger Syrup

Preparation time: 15 minutes
Cooking time: 55 minutes
Servings: 10

Ingredients:

1 cup Ginger, sliced thinly
1 large White Onion, peeled
2 ½ cups Water
¼ cup Sugar

Instructions:

1. Make a water bath, place a Sous Vide cooker in it, and set it at 185 °F. Place the onion in a vacuum-sealable bag.
2. Release air by the water displacement method, seal and submerge the bag in the water bath. Set the timer for 40 minutes.
3. Once the timer has stopped, remove and unseal the bag.
4. Transfer the onion with 4 tablespoons of water to a blender and puree to smooth.
5. Place a pot over medium heat, add the onion puree and the remaining listed ingredients. Bring to a boil for 15 minutes.
6. Turn off heat, cool, and strain through a fine sieve.
7. Store in a jar, refrigerate and use for up to 14 days. Use it as a spice in other foods.

Nutrition facts per serving: Calories 32, Total Fat 0g, Sodium 10mg, Potassium 6mg, Total Carbs 8.3g, Net Carbs 8.1g, Protein 0.1

Chili & Garlic Sauce

Preparation time: 7 minutes
Cooking time: 30 minutes
Servings: 15

Ingredients:

2 lb Red Chili Peppers

4 cloves Garlic, crushed

2 tsp Smoked Paprika

1 cup Cilantro Leaves, chopped

½ cup Basil Leaves, chopped

1 cup Olive Oil

2 Lemons' Juice

Instructions:

1. Make a water bath, place a Sous Vide cooker in it, and set it at 185 °F.
2. Place the peppers in a vacuum-sealable bag.
3. Release air by the water displacement method, seal and submerge the bag in the water bath. Set the timer for 30 minutes.
4. Once the timer has stopped, remove and unseal the bag.
5. Transfer the pepper and the remaining listed ingredients to a blender and puree to smooth.
6. Store in an airtight container, refrigerate and use for up to 7 days.

Nutrition facts per serving: Calories 25, Total Fat 0.2g, Sodium 4mg, Potassium 216mg, Total Carbs 5.6g, Net Carbs 5.6g, Protein 0.9g

Homemade Jalapeno Seasoning

Preparation time: 5 minutes
Cooking time: 55 minutes
Servings: 6

Ingredients:

2 Jalapeno Peppers
2 Green Chili Peppers
2 cloves Garlic, crushed
1 medium Onion, peeled only
3 tsp Oregano Powder
3 tsp Black Pepper Powder
2 tsp Rosemary Powder
10 tsp Aniseed Powder

Instructions

1. Make a water bath, place a Sous Vide cooker in it, and set it at 185 F. Place the peppers and onion in a vacuum-sealable bag.

2. Release air by the water displacement method, seal and submerge the bag in the water bath. Set the timer for 40 minutes. Once the timer has stopped, remove and unseal the bag. Transfer the pepper and onion with 2 tablespoons of water to a blender and puree to smooth.

3. Place a pot over low heat, add the pepper puree and the remaining listed ingredients. Simmer for 15 minutes. Turn off heat and cool.

4. Store in a spice jar, refrigerate and use for up to 7 days. Use it as a spice in other foods.

Nutrition facts per serving: Calories 2, Total Fat 0g, Sodium 72mg, Potassium 248mg, Carbs 0g, Protein 0.9g

Made in the USA
Monee, IL
08 December 2019